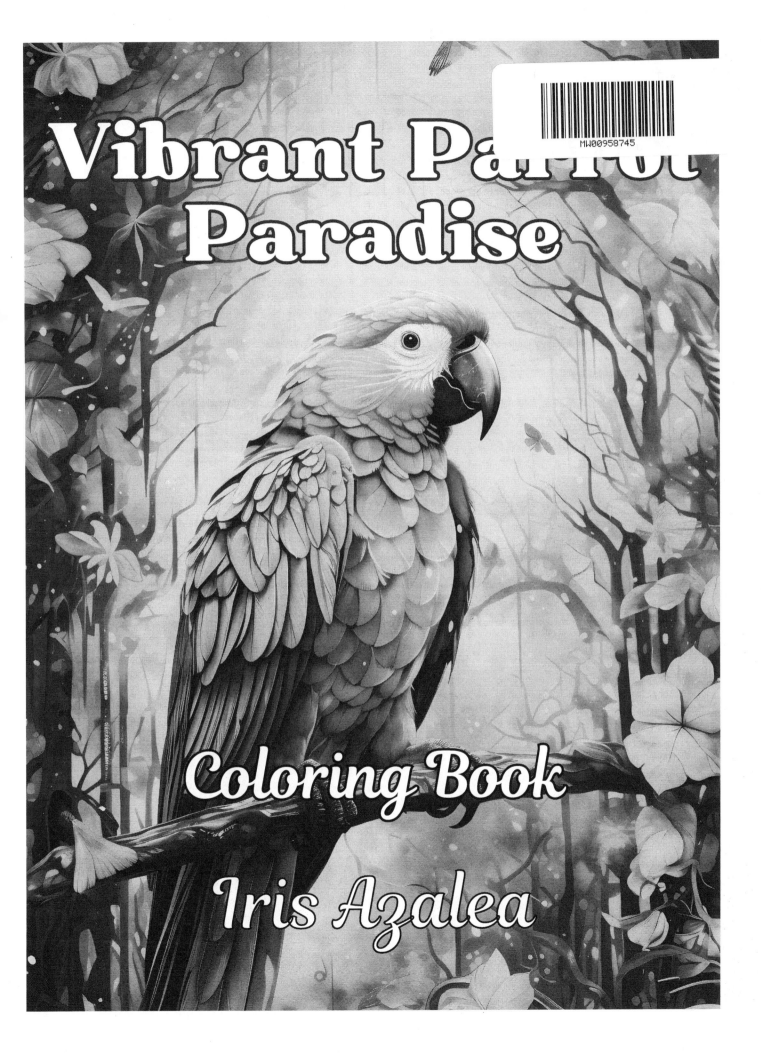

Vibrant Parrot Paradise

Coloring Book

Iris Azalea

THIS BOOK BELONGS TO

. . . .

COLORING TIPS

Thank you for purchasing this colouring book. Inside you will find 50 Inspirational and Magical Parrots for you to relax, color and explore your creativity.

Each page has a blank side for potential bleed through with wet pens.

If you are using wet pens, please insert a blank page behind the page you are working on to prevent bleed through to the next coloring page.

You can test you colors on the Test pages in the front and back of this book.

I hope you enjoy this coloring book and would appreciate a review to help me as an independent publisher.

Happy Coloring

Iris Azalea

Color Test Page

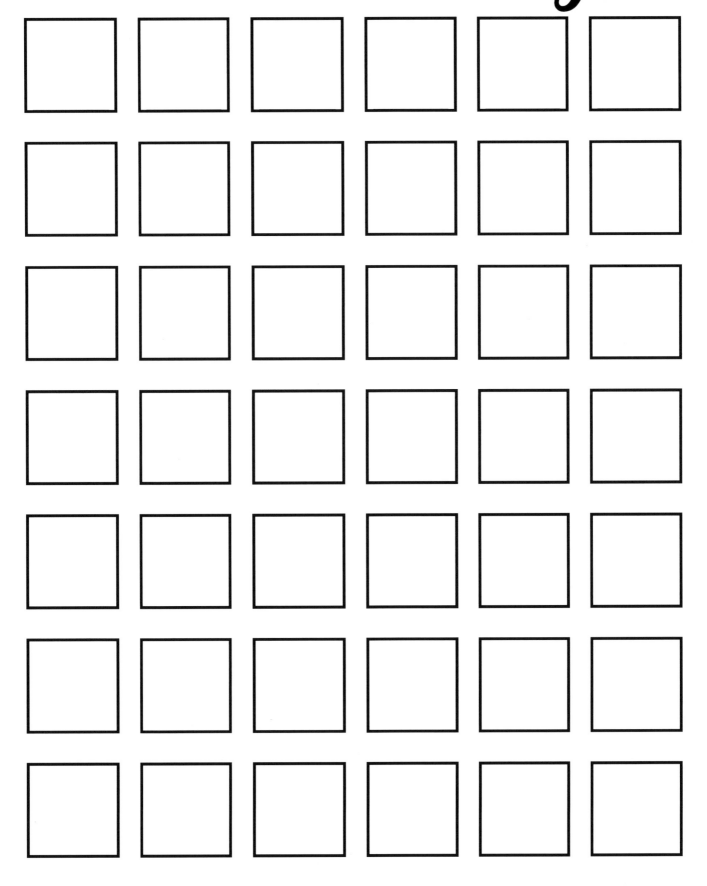

Color Test Page

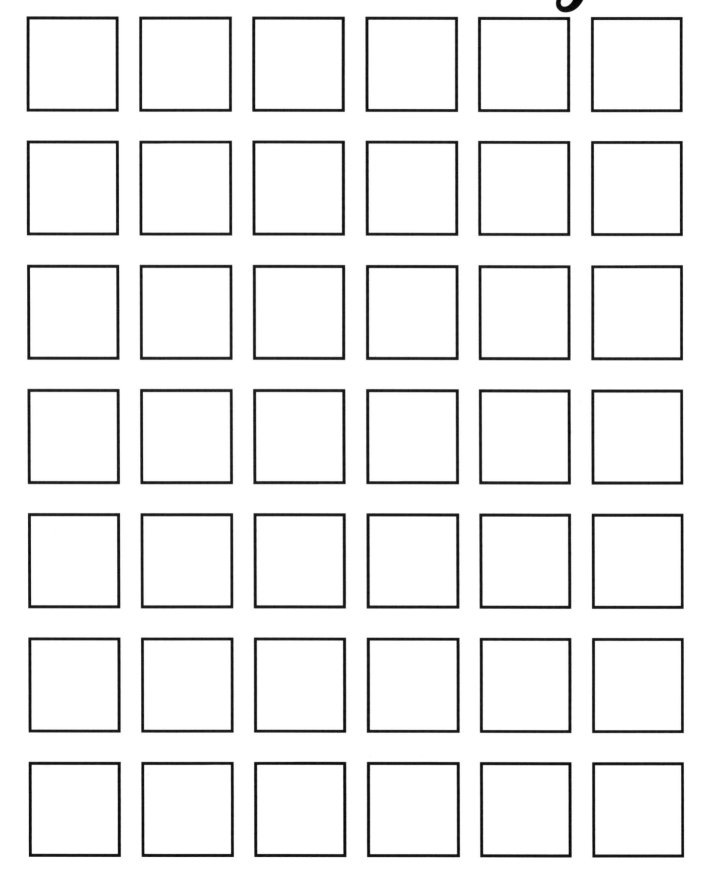

Other books you will enjoy by Iris Azalea

(Just type in the ASIN number in the Amazon Search bar or look through my Author page)

ASIN: B0C91NT8XV

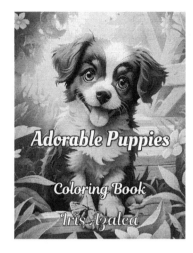

ASIN: B0CCCMWD4Q

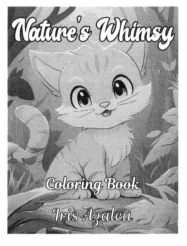

ASIN: B0C91RTZK6

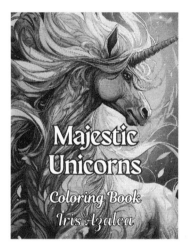

ASIN: B0CH2NT98Z

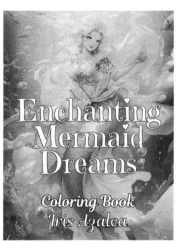

ASIN: B0CH2D5JLV

ASIN: B0C91HLBQ1

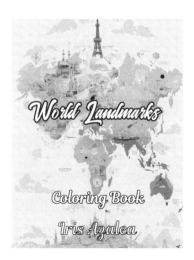

ASIN: B0C9S57DBY

ASIN: B0CCCQYNY6

ASIN: B0CCCHSHH5